THIS JOURNAL BELONGS TO:

(STEAL LIKE AN ARTIST,
NOT A JERK)

THE
STEAL
LIKE AN
ARTIST
JOURNAL

A NOTEBOOK FOR CREATIVE KLEPTOMANIACS

AUSTIN KLEON

WORKMAN PUBLISHING · NEW YORK

Library of Congress Cataloging-in-Publication Data is available.

ISBN 978-0-7611-8568-0

Design by Becky Terhune

Workman books are available at special discounts when purchased in bulk for
premiums and sales promotions as well as for fund-raising or educational use.
Special editions or book excerpts also can be created to specification.
For details, contact the Special Sales Director at the address below,
or send an email to specialmarkets@workman.com.

Workman Publishing Co., Inc.
225 Varick Street
New York, NY 10014-4381
workman.com

Printed in China
First printing September 2015

10 9 8 7 6 5 4 3

"I think we're creative all day long.
We have to have an appointment
to have that work out on the page.
Because the creative part of us gets
tired of waiting, or just gets tired."

—*Mary Oliver*

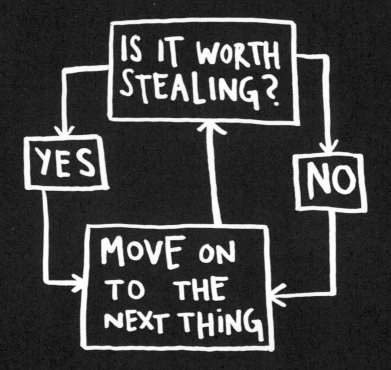

HOW TO BE A CREATIVE KLEPTOMANIAC

"Art is theft."

—*Pablo Picasso*

This journal is designed to get you looking at your world like an artist, always "casing the joint," always collecting ideas, always looking for the next bit of inspiration to lift—to turn you into a creative kleptomanic.

Great artists, scientists, entrepreneurs, and anyone else who has done successful creative work understands that nothing comes from nowhere. Everything builds on what came before, and every new idea is just a mashup or a remix of one or more previous ideas. Nothing is completely original.

GOOD THEFT	VS.	BAD THEFT
HONOR		DEGRADE
STUDY		SKIM
STEAL FROM MANY		STEAL FROM ONE
CREDIT		PLAGIARIZE
TRANSFORM		IMITATE
REMIX		RIP OFF

> "Immature poets imitate; mature poets steal; bad poets deface what they take, and good poets make it into something better, or at least something different. The good poet welds his theft into a whole of feeling which is unique, utterly different from that from which it was torn."
>
> —*T. S. Eliot*

If we're free from the burden of trying to be completely original, we can stop trying to make something out of nothing, and we can embrace influence instead of running away from it.

Your job, then, becomes to collect good ideas. The more good ideas you collect, the more you can choose from to be influenced by.

Some of the best minds on the planet used notebooks to collect ideas: Charles Darwin, Pablo Picasso, Virginia Woolf, Ludwig van Beethoven, Marie Curie, Thomas Edison, Leonardo da Vinci, Frida Kahlo . . . the list goes on and on.

Follow their example, and make this notebook part of your everyday life.

Carry it with you everywhere you go. Get used to pulling it out and jotting down your thoughts and observations in the blank pages. Set aside fifteen minutes every day to do one of the exercises. (Commutes or lunch breaks are perfect.) Make it yours—if you hate one of the exercises, cross out the prompt and come up with one of your own. Flip back through it when you need ideas.

By the time all these pages are full, you'll have learned how to look at your influences and your everyday life as raw material for your work. You'll be ready to take what you've stolen, turn it into work of your own, and release it back into the world, so we can steal from you.

> **"We are all having ideas all the time. But I'm on the lookout for them. You're not."**
>
> *—Philip Pullman*

HOW TO USE
THIS JOURNAL

① CARRY IT WITH YOU
   WHEREVER YOU GO.

② DO AT LEAST ONE
   EXERCISE EVERY DAY.

③ REPEAT THE FIRST TWO
   STEPS UNTIL THE PAGES
   ARE FULL.

10 THINGS I WANT TO LEARN:

1.

2.

3.

4.

5.

6.

7.

8.

9.

10.

PICTURES CAN SAY WHATEVER WE WANT THEM TO SAY.

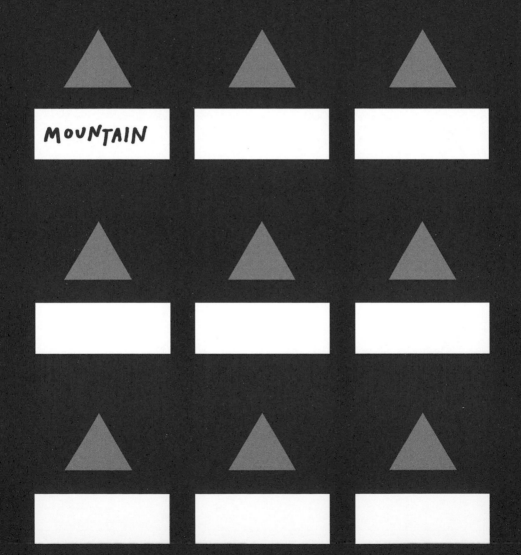

MOUNTAIN

GO TO AN ART STORE AND SHOP FOR A NEW PEN.
USE THIS PAGE AS A TESTER.

KERI SMITH

STEAL A TITLE FROM A BOOK YOU'VE NEVER
READ AND INVENT YOUR OWN STORY.

30-DAY CHALLENGE

EVERY DAY, I WILL ⬜

AND AFTER I DO, I WILL PUT AN X IN THE BOX.

1	2	3	4	5	6
7	8	9	10	11	12
13	14	15	16	17	18
19	20	21	22	23	24
25	26	27	28	29	30

I WILL NOT BREAK THE CHAIN.

AFTER 30 DAYS, I GET ⬜

WRITE A FAN LETTER.

MAKE A MIXTAPE

FOR SOMEONE WHO DOESN'T KNOW YOU.

(A)

(B)

THANKS TO _____

WHO TAUGHT ME _____

_____ .

THANKS TO _____

WHO TAUGHT ME _____

_____ .

THANKS TO _____

WHO TAUGHT ME _____

_____ .

THANKS TO _____

WHO TAUGHT ME _____

_____ .

THANKS TO _____

WHO TAUGHT ME _____

_____ .

STACK BOOKS. MAKE A POEM OUT OF
THE SPINES. DRAW THE STACK.

NINA KATCHADOURIAN

COPY A PASSAGE FROM ONE OF YOUR FAVORITE BOOKS.
WRITE AS S L O W L Y AS YOU CAN STAND.

FILL THE SPEECH BALLOONS.

COLOR THE BACKGROUNDS.

FILL THIS PAGE WITH DOODLES UNTIL YOU GET AN IDEA.

FIND A RECEIPT AND PASTE IT HERE.

Little Deli
7101-A Woodrow Ave.
Austin, TX 78757

Server: Bobbie   Station: 6

Order #: 579769   HERE ORDER
Customer Name: austin
----
1 Harrys Perfect   13.30
  z---SPLIT---z
2 Soft Drink   4.00

SUB TOTAL: 17.30
Sales Tax: 1.43
                                    ==========
TOTAL: $18.73

Visa Tendered: 18.73

                                    ==========
CHANGE: 0.00

          10/29/2014 11:05:01 AM

            THANK YOU!

FILL THIS PAGE WITH WHAT YOU CAN REMEMBER ABOUT THE DAY YOU MADE THE PURCHASE.

START RANDOMLY TYPING INTO A SEARCH BOX
AND WRITE DOWN THE AUTO SUGGESTIONS.

"D'ye see him?" cried Ahab, after allowing a little space for the light to spread.

"See nothing, sir."

"Turn up all hands and make sail! he travels faster than I thought for;—the top-gallant sails!—aye, they should have been kept on her all night. But no matter—'tis but resting for the rush."

Here be it said, that this pertinacious pursuit of one particular whale, continued through day into night, and through night into day, is a thing by no means unprecedented in the South sea fishery. For such is the wonderful skill, prescience of experience, and invincible confidence acquired by some great natural geniuses among the Nantucket commanders; that from the simple observation of a whale when last descried, they will, under certain given circumstances, pretty accurately foretell both the direction in which he will continue to swim for a time, while out of sight, as well as his probable rate of progression during that period. And, in these cases, somewhat as a pilot, when about losing sight of a coast, whose general trending he well knows, and which he desires shortly to return to again, but at some further point; like as this pilot stands by his compass, and takes the precise bearing of the cape at present visible, in order the more certainly to hit aright the remote, unseen headland, eventually to be visited: so does the fisherman, at his compass, with the whale; for after being chased, and diligently marked, through several hours of daylight, then, when night obscures the fish, the creature's future wake through the darkness is almost as established to the sagacious mind of the hunter, as the pilot's coast is to him. So that to this hunter's wondrous skill, the proverbial evanescence of a thing writ in water, a wake, is to all desired purposes well nigh as reliable as the steadfast land. And as the mighty iron Leviathan of the modern railway is so familiarly known in its every pace, that, with watches in their hands, men time his rate as doctors that of a baby's pulse; and lightly say of it, the up train or the down train will reach such or such a spot, at such or such an hour; even so, almost, there are occasions when these Nantucketers time that other Leviathan of the deep, according to the observed humor of his speed; and say to themselves, so many hours hence this whale will have gone two hundred miles, will have about reached this or that degree of latitude or longitude. But to render this acuteness at all successful in the end, the wind and the sea must be the whaleman's allies; for of what present avail to the becalmed or windbound mariner is the skill that assures him he is exactly ninety-three leagues and a quarter from his port? Inferable from these statements, are many collateral subtile matters touching the chase of whales.

The ship tore on; leaving such a furrow in the sea as when a cannon-ball, missent, becomes a plough-share and turns up the level field.

"By salt and hemp!" cried Stubb, "but this swift motion of the deck creeps up one's legs and tingles at the heart. This ship and I are two brave fellows!—Ha! ha! Some one take me up, and launch me, spine-wise, on the sea,—for by live-oaks! my spine's a keel. Ha, ha! we go the gait that leaves no dust behind!"

"There she blows—she blows!—she blows!—right ahead!" was now the mast-head cry.

"Aye, aye!" cried Stubb, "I knew it—ye can't escape—blow on and split your spout, O whale! the mad fiend himself is after ye! blow your trump—blister your lungs!—Ahab will dam off your blood, as a miller shuts his water-gate upon the stream!"

And Stubb did but speak out for well nigh all that crew. The frenzies of the chase had by this time worked them bubblingly up, like old wine worked anew. Whatever pale fears and forebodings some of them might have felt before; these were not only now kept out of sight through the growing awe

DRAW A MAP OF YOUR TYPICAL WEEK.

(IS IT SMALLER OR BIGGER THAN YOU THOUGHT IT'D BE?)

RECENT VICTORIES	RECENT LOSSES

WRITE DOWN EVERYTHING YOU ARE AFRAID OF:

NOW CROSS EACH ONE OUT AS IF SLAYING A DRAGON WITH A SWORD.

10 THINGS LYING AROUND THAT NOBODY'S USING:

1.

2.

3.

4.

5.

6.

7.

8.

9.

10.

MAKE A CUP OF TEA. SET THE USED TEA BAG
ON A PIECE OF PAPER. WHAT DOES THE STAIN
REMIND YOU OF?

DAVE GRAY TEA STAIN   🔍

EAVESDROP ON A CONVERSATION.

CUT OUT THE PANELS IN A COMIC STRIP, REARRANGE THEM, AND PASTE THEM HERE.

WHAT EXCITES YOU?	WHAT DRAINS YOU?
(DO MORE OF THIS)	(DO LESS OF THIS)

<u>BACKWARDS</u> IT WRITE BUT BOOKS FAVORITE
YOUR OF ONE FROM PASSAGE A COPY

FOR ONE WEEK, SIT OR STAND IN THE SAME SPOT
FOR 15 MINUTES EVERY DAY. EACH DAY, WRITE
DOWN THE MOST INTERESTING THING YOU SEE
OR HEAR.

THE SPOT:

MONDAY	
TUESDAY	
WEDNESDAY	

THURSDAY	
FRIDAY	
SATURDAY	
SUNDAY	

WITHOUT ANY HELP, TRANSLATE A PARAGRAPH
FROM A LANGUAGE YOU DON'T SPEAK.
TRY TO BE AS ACCURATE AS YOU CAN.

WRITE DOWN YOUR DREAMS
FIRST THING EVERY MORNING.

KEEP THIS PAGE OPEN BY YOUR BED UNTIL IT IS FULL.

ASK THE PERSON NEAREST TO YOU WHAT YOU SHOULD DO WITH THIS PAGE.

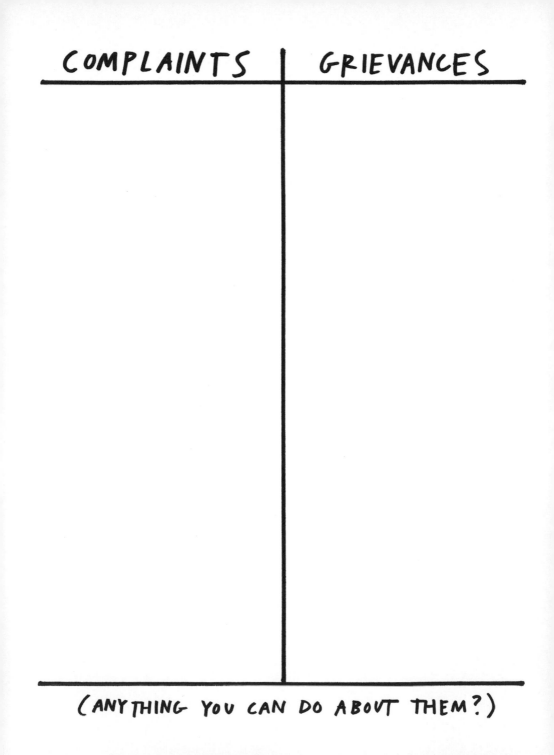

COMPLAINTS	GRIEVANCES

(ANYTHING YOU CAN DO ABOUT THEM?)

TURN ON A RADIO. SWITCH THE STATION EVERY
10 SECONDS. TRANSCRIBE EVERYTHING YOU HEAR.

CLIMB UP YOUR OWN

WHO WAS
INFLUENCED
BY

I AM MOST
INFLUENCED BY

CREATIVE FAMILY TREE.

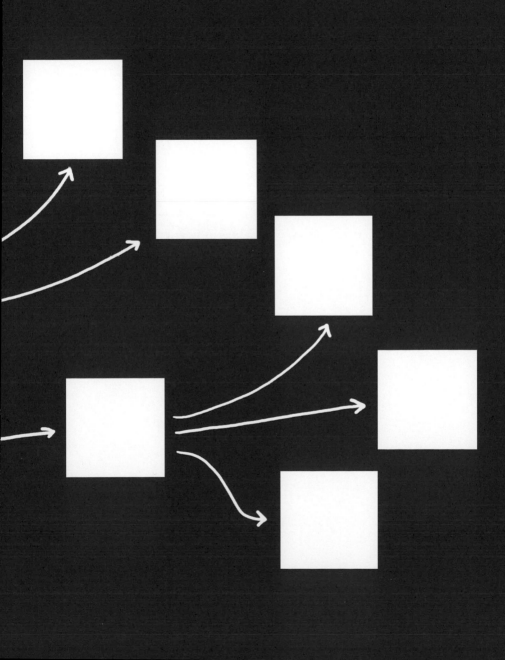

ASK SOMEBODY TO COFFEE.
AFTERWARD, WRITE DOWN EVERYTHING YOU REMEMBER ABOUT THE CONVERSATION.

PRACTICE FORGING A SIGNATURE.

_____

_____

_____

_____

_____

_____

_____

_____

_____

MAKE A COLLAGE FROM ITEMS IN YOUR WASTEBASKET.

(OPTIONAL: STEAL SCRAPS FROM SOMEONE ELSE'S WASTEBASKET.)

WHAT ARE YOU HOARDING FOR YOURSELF
THAT COULD BE SHARED WITH OTHERS?

WRITE YOUR FAVORITE QUOTE HERE:

SAY IT 5 DIFFERENT WAYS:

①

②

③

④

⑤

Make a Poem out OF Newspaper headlines

TRACE A SHADOW.

MAKE A DRAWING USING TINY PARTS
OF OTHER PEOPLE'S DRAWINGS.

10 THINGS I COULD'VE DONE BUT DIDN'T:

1.

2.

3.

4.

5.

6.

7.

8.

9.

10.

RESEARCH AN "OVERNIGHT SUCCESS"
STORY. WAS IT TRULY OVERNIGHT?

WRITE SOMETHING HERE THAT WOULD GET YOU
FIRED, EXPELLED, OR DISOWNED:

(SCRIBBLE OVER IT SO NOBODY CAN EVER READ IT.)

ONCE UPON A TIME

THERE WAS _____

_____

_____

EVERY DAY _____

_____

_____

ONE DAY _____

_____

_____

BECAUSE OF THAT _____

_____

_____

UNTIL FINALLY _____

_____

_____

EMMA COATS PIXAR FAIRY TALE 🔍

WATCH A TV SHOW WITH THE SOUND MUTED.
INVENT YOUR OWN DIALOGUE.

(TRY A SOAP OPERA.)

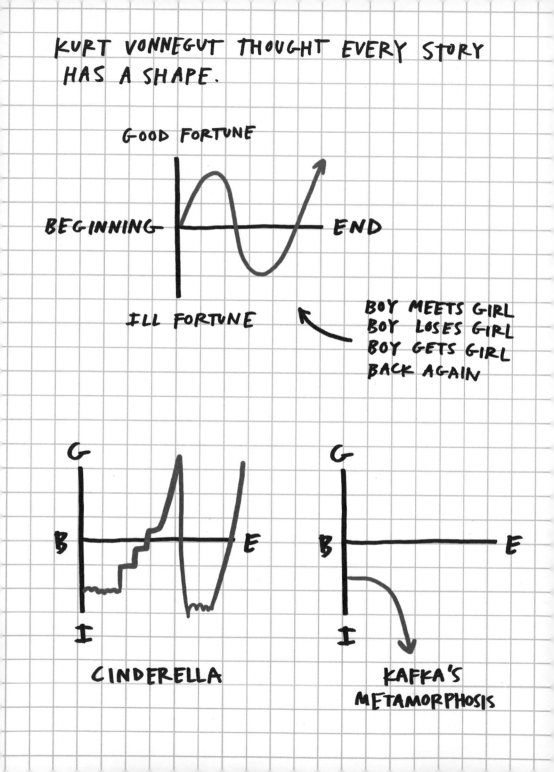

KURT VONNEGUT THOUGHT EVERY STORY HAS A SHAPE.

GOOD FORTUNE

BEGINNING — END

ILL FORTUNE

BOY MEETS GIRL
BOY LOSES GIRL
BOY GETS GIRL
BACK AGAIN

CINDERELLA

KAFKA'S METAMORPHOSIS

GRAPH A COUPLE OF YOUR FAVORITE STORIES.

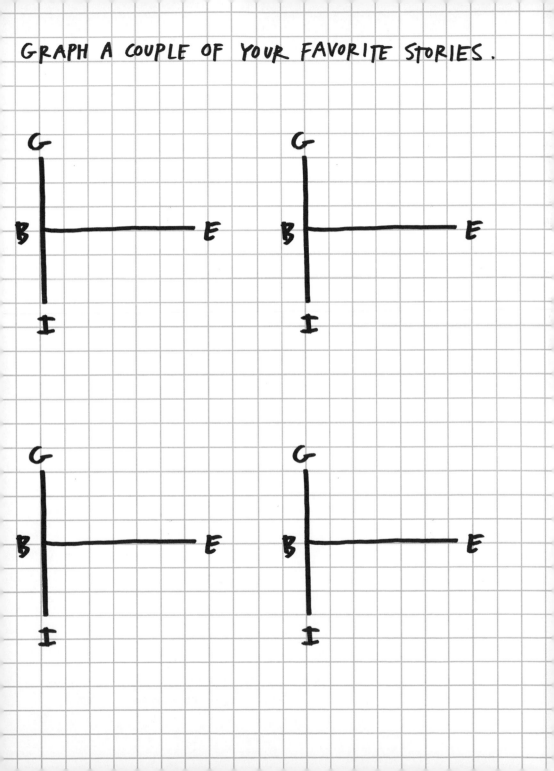

STARE AT THIS DOT
UNTIL YOU GET AN IDEA

WRITE A LETTER TO SOMEONE YOU HATE.
TRY TO MAKE THEM LAUGH.

MAKE UP 10 PSEUDONYMS FOR YOURSELF:

1.

2.

3.

4.

5.

6.

7.

8.

9.

10.

WHEN WAS THE LAST TIME YOU REALLY HAD FUN?

PICK A COLOR. GO TO THE BOOKSTORE AND
WRITE DOWN THE TITLES OF THE FIRST 10
BOOK COVERS YOU SEE WITH THAT COLOR.

1.

2.

3.

4.

5.

6.

7.

8.

9.

10.

(OPTIONAL: READ THE BOOKS.)

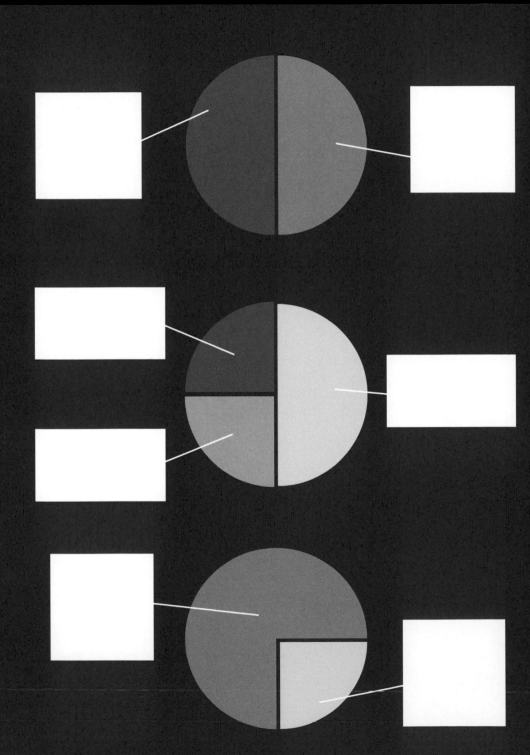

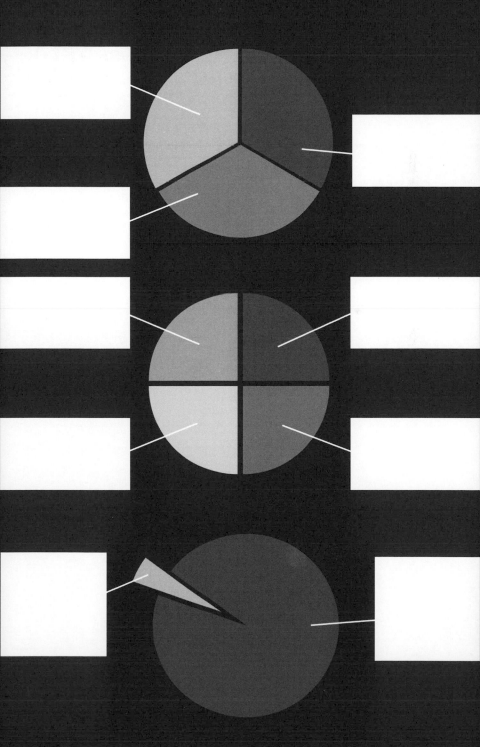

TAKE A WALK ON YOUR LUNCH BREAK.
LIST EVERYTHING YOU HEAR, SEE, OR THINK.

MY TOP 10 GUILTY PLEASURES:

1.

2.

3.

4.

5.

6.

7.

8.

9.

10.

"I DON'T BELIEVE IN GUILTY PLEASURES. IF YOU F***ING LIKE SOMETHING, LIKE IT." —DAVE GROHL

DRAW A PICTURE OF YOUR WORKSPACE.

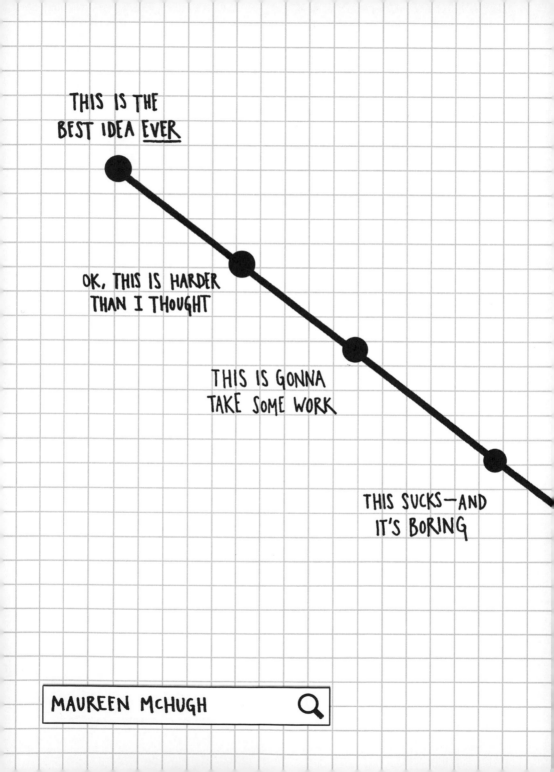

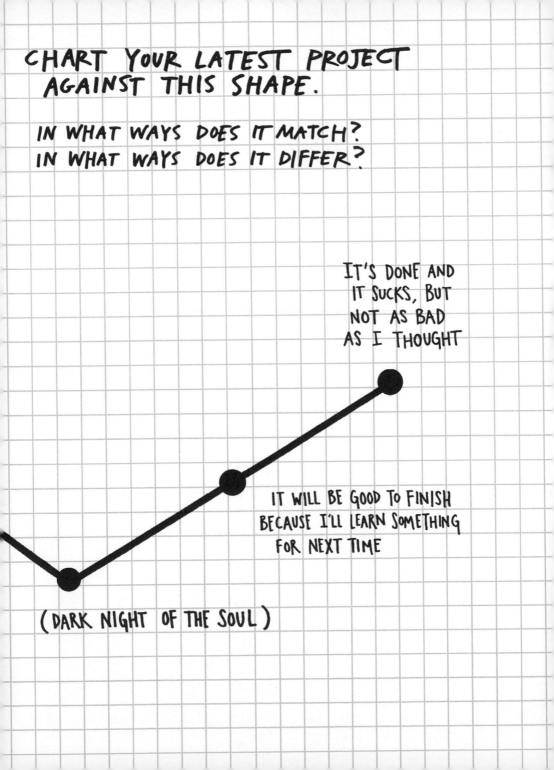

DESCRIBE YOUR FAVORITE METHOD OF PROCRASTINATION.
CAN YOU COME UP WITH A MORE PRODUCTIVE ONE?

DESCRIBE WHAT YOU DO IN SIX WORDS.

I   AM   A   WRITER   WHO   DRAWS
_____ _____ _____ _____ _____ _____

I   AM   A   WHO
_____ _____ _____ _____ _____ _____

_____ _____ _____ _____ _____ _____

_____ _____ _____ _____ _____ _____

I   HELP
_____ _____ _____ _____ _____ _____

_____ _____ _____ _____ _____ _____

_____ _____ _____ _____ _____ _____

"SIT AT YOUR DESK AND LISTEN."
—FRANZ KAFKA

WHAT ARE THE SECRETS OF YOUR TRADE?
WHAT WOULD YOU LOSE BY SHARING THEM WITH OTHERS?
WHAT WOULD YOU GAIN?

DRAW A COMIC WHERE EACH PANEL...

10 QUESTIONS I HAVE:

1.

2.

3.

4.

5.

6.

7.

8.

9.

10.

WHAT ARE YOU THINKING THAT NOBODY ELSE IS SAYING?

MAKE UP A REALLY GOOD LIE ABOUT YOURSELF TO TELL
A STRANGER. INVENT A STORY TO BACK IT UP.

GET A HAIRCUT. RECALL YOUR CONVERSATION WITH YOUR BARBER OR HAIRDRESSER.

10 THINGS I PROBABLY THINK ABOUT MORE THAN THE AVERAGE PERSON :

1.

2.

3.

4.

5.

6.

7.

8.

9.

10.

TAKE A LONG, HOT SHOWER OR A BATH.
FILL THIS PAGE WHEN YOU'RE DONE.

NEGATIVE MANIFESTO:

I WILL NOT _____

_____

I WILL NOT _____

_____

I WILL NOT _____

_____

I WILL NOT _____

_____

I WILL NOT _____

_____

I WILL NOT _____

_____

I WILL NOT _____

_____

COPY A FAVORITE SENTENCE ONTO THE MIDDLE OF THIS PAGE.
WRITE TWO OF YOUR OWN SENTENCES THAT LEAD UP TO IT.
WRITE TWO OF YOUR OWN SENTENCES THAT FOLLOW IT.

THEN CROSS OUT THE ORIGINAL SENTENCE.

MAKE A PHONE CALL. DIAGRAM THE CONVERSATION.

GO TO THE MOVIES. DRAW IN THE DARK.

WHO DO YOU TRUST WITH YOUR SECRETS?
WHY?

10 THINGS THAT ARE GOING GREAT RIGHT NOW:

1.

2.

3.

4.

5.

6.

7.

8.

9.

10.

WHO DO YOU FEEL ARE YOUR COMPETITORS?
COULD YOU TURN THEM INTO COLLABORATORS? HOW?

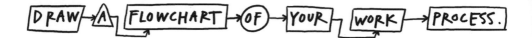

DRAW → A → FLOWCHART → OF → YOUR → WORK → PROCESS.

(FEEL FREE TO MAKE IT FUNNY.)

WHAT ARE YOU REALLY WORKING ON?

$1 + 1 = 3$

JAWS	+	SPACE	=	ALIEN
FLICKR	+	VIDEO	=	YOUTUBE
	+		=	
	+		=	
	+		=	
	+		=	
	+		=	

MAKE A FAKE ADVERTISEMENT FOR
A PRODUCT YOU'D LIKE TO EXIST.

TAKE A NAP.

FILL THIS PAGE WHEN YOU WAKE UP.

WRITE DOWN YOUR BEST IDEA.

HOW DO YOU FEEL ABOUT IT AFTER 24 HOURS?

A WEEK?

A MONTH?

WHAT DO YOU DO IN PRIVATE THAT COULD BE DONE IN PUBLIC? WHY DON'T YOU?

PLAGIARIZE YOURSELF.
FIND AN OLD PIECE OF WRITING, CUT IT UP, REARRANGE IT, AND PASTE IT HERE.

MY TOP TEN _____

1.

2.

3.

4.

5.

6.

7.

8.

9.

10.

FLIP BACK THROUGH THIS LOGBOOK.
DO YOU DETECT ANY THEMES OR PATTERNS?

GOOGLE A PROBLEM YOU HAVE.
WRITE DOWN THE RESULTS WITHOUT EDITING.

THE BEST THING THAT HAPPENED YESTERDAY:

LAST MONTH:

IN THE PAST YEAR:

IN MY LIFE:

TAKE A ONE-DAY VOW OF SILENCE.
USE YOUR PEN AND THIS PAGE TO RESPOND TO OTHERS.

HOW ARE YOU KEEPING YOUR NAME CLEAN?

FIND AN OLD PHOTO
AND PASTE IT HERE.

COME UP WITH 10 DIFFERENT CAPTIONS.
MAKE HALF FUNNY, HALF SAD.

①

②

③

④

⑤

⑥

⑦

⑧

⑨

⑩

TRACE A FRIEND'S SILHOUETTE. FILL IT WITH WORDS.

SPEND $5 AT THE SCHOOL SUPPLY AISLE IN THE GROCERY STORE. MAKE SOMETHING HERE THAT YOUR MOM WOULD PUT ON THE REFRIGERATOR.

WHAT DID YOU WANT TO DO WHEN YOU WERE ELEVEN?

INVENT A RECIPE.

TITLE:

INGREDIENTS:

DIRECTIONS:

PREP TIME:

WRITE YOUR OBITUARY.

(OPTIONAL: WRITE YOUR OBIT USING NOTHING BUT SENTENCES FROM OBITS IN THE PAPER.)

WHAT'S SOMETHING YOU'VE DISCARDED THAT YOU MISS? WHY?

TITLE:

DESCRIPTION:

GOALS:

CLASSROOM RULES:

REQUIRED TEXTS AND/OR MATERIALS:

SCHEDULE

DATE	LESSON

THE WORLD IS ENDING.
LEAVE A MESSAGE FOR ALIEN EXPLORERS.

10 THINGS I'VE LEARNED:

1.

2.

3.

4.

5.

6.

7.

8.

9.

10.

WHAT NOW?

- KEEP UP THE HABIT! WHEN THESE PAGES ARE FULL, START A NEW NOTEBOOK AND CARRY IT WITH YOU EVERYWHERE.

- SHOW YOUR WORK! IF THERE'S A PAGE IN YOUR JOURNAL THAT YOU THINK WOULD BE INTERESTING OR HELPFUL TO OTHERS, TAKE A PICTURE AND POST IT ONLINE WITH THE TAG #STEALJOURNAL.

- PLAN A JOURNALING MEETUP WITH FRIENDS, FAMILY, CLASSMATES, OR COLLEAGUES. PICK A PAGE FROM THIS NOTEBOOK, SET A TIMER, AND ANSWER THE PROMPT. SHARE YOUR RESULTS WITH EACH OTHER.

- GIVE A COPY OF THIS JOURNAL TO SOMEBODY WHO COULD USE IT!

BOOKS TO READ

- [ ] KENT + STEWARD, <u>LEARNING BY HEART</u>
- [ ]
- [ ]
- [ ]
- [ ]
- [ ]
- [ ]
- [ ]
- [ ]
- [ ]
- [ ]
- [ ]
- [ ]

MOVIES TO SEE

- [ ] BEAUTY IS EMBARRASSING
- [ ]
- [ ]
- [ ]
- [ ]
- [ ]
- [ ]
- [ ]
- [ ]
- [ ]
- [ ]
- [ ]
- [ ]

MUSIC TO LISTEN TO

☐ CURTIS MAYFIELD, CURTIS/LIVE!

☐

☐

☐

☐

☐

☐

☐

☐

☐

☐

☐

☐

I'VE BEEN KEEPING A NOTEBOOK FOR
20 YEARS — ALMOST 2/3 OF MY LIFE.

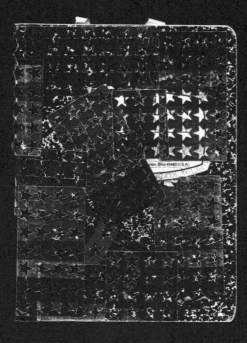

I HOPE THE HABIT TREATS YOU AS WELL AS IT HAS TREATED ME.

NEED MORE INSPIRATION?

EVERY WEEK I SEND OUT A NEWSLETTER
FILLED WITH NEW ART, WRITING,
AND INTERESTING LINKS.

SIGN UP HERE TO SUBSCRIBE:
AUSTINKLEON.COM

FOR DAILY UPDATES, FOLLOW ME ON TWITTER:
@AUSTINKLEON